WORLD WAR I
1914–1916
A Terrible New Warfare Begins

JANE H. GOULD

Crabtree Publishing Company
www.crabtreebooks.com

WORLD WAR I
Remembering the Great War

Author: Jane H. Gould
Editor: Lynn Peppas
Proofreaders: Lisa Slone, Wendy Scavuzzo
Editorial director: Kathy Middleton
Production coordinator: Shivi Sharma
Design concept: Margaret Amy Salter
Cover design: Ken Wright
Photo research: Nivisha Sinha, Crystal Sikkens
Maps: Contentra Technologies
Production coordinator and
Prepress technician: Ken Wright
Print coordinator: Katherine Berti

Written, developed, and produced by
Contentra Technologies

Cover: German soldiers wearing gas masks in
their trench
Title page: The French (in blue) are defending
a hill against German troops at the Battle of
Verdun, 1916
Contents page: A German long-range gun used
to bombarded Paris, France.

Photo Credits:
Alamy: 16 (© GL Archive), 18 (© Lebrecht Music and Arts Photo Library), 19 (© The Art Archive), 21 (© DIZ Muenchen GmbH, Sueddeutsche Zeitung Photo), 24b (PENDING), 27 (© Pictorial Press Ltd), 30t (© The Keasbury-Gordon Photograph Archive), 36 (© The Art Archive), 37 (© Classic Image), 38 (© Lordprice Collection), 43 (© Photos 12)
The Bridgeman Art Library: 5 ('Over the Top' 1st Artists' Rifles at Marcoing, 30th December 1917, 1918 (oil on canvas), Nash, John Northcote (1893–1977)/Imperial War Museum, London, UK/© IWM (Art.IWM ART 1656)), 10 (Homeless (colour litho), Jack, Richard (1866–1952) (after)/Private Collection/Peter Newark Military Pictures), 32 (Sinking of the Lusitania, Smith, John S. (20th century)/Private Collection/© Look and Learn), 33 (The Battle of Jutland, 1916 (oil on canvas), Smith, Robert H. (20th century)/Private Collection/Topham Picturepoint), 35 (L'Enfer (Hell), 1921 (oil on canvas), Leroux, Georges Paul (1877–1957)/Imperial War Museum, London, UK), 42 (Japanese siege gun in action against the German fortress of Tsingtao on the China coast, 1914 (photo), Japanese Photographer (20th century)/Private Collection/Peter Newark Pictures)
Corbis: 23 (© Bettmann)
Getty Images: 15 (Hulton Archive), 17 (Popperfoto), 22 (Hulton Archive), 24t (Print Collector), 30b (Hulton Archive), 34 (IWM via Getty Images)
© SZ Photo / Scherl / The Image Works: 25
© Imperial War Museums (INS 6062): Content Page, 8
India Picture: 12 (Mary Evans/Sueddeutsche Zeitung Photo), 14 (Heritage Images), 28 (Mary Evans/Sueddeutsche Zeitung Photo), 40 (©)Robert Hunt Library/Mary Evans)
Library of Congress: 4 (LC-USZC4-10987), 11 (LC-DIG-ggbain-17434), 31 (LC-USZ62-93699)
Cover: De Agostini Picture Library / The Bridgeman Art Library
Title: Roger Viollet/Getty Images
Back cover: Wikimedia Commons: Library and Archives Canada (background) Shutterstock: I. Pilon (medals); Shuttertock: IanC66 (airplane)

t=Top, b=Bottom, l=Left, r=Right

Library and Archives Canada Cataloguing in Publication

Gould, Jane H., 1956-, author
World War I : 1914-1916 : a terrible new warfare begins / Jane H. Gould.

(World War I : remembering the Great War)
Includes index.
Issued in print and electronic formats.
ISBN 978-0-7787-0325-9 (bound).--ISBN 978-0-7787-0390-7 (pbk.).--ISBN 978-1-4271-7502-1 (pdf).--ISBN 978-1-4271-7496-3 (html)

1. World War, 1914-1918--Trench warfare--Juvenile literature. 2. World War, 1914-1918--Campaigns--Western Front--Juvenile literature. I. Title. II. Title: World War One. III. Title: World War 1. IV. Title: Terrible new warfare begins.

D530.G68 2014   j940.4'144   C2014-903260-9
                                                C2014-903261-7

Library of Congress Cataloging-in-Publication Data

Gould, Jane H.
World War I, 1914-1916 : a terrible new warfare begins / Jane H. Gould.
pages cm. -- (World War I: remembering the Great War)
Includes index.
ISBN 978-0-7787-0325-9 (reinforced library binding : alk. paper) -- ISBN 978-0-7787-0390-7 (pbk. : alk. paper) -- ISBN 978-1-4271-7502-1 (electronic pdf : alk. paper) -- ISBN 978-1-4271-7496-3 (electronic html : alk. paper)
1. World War, 1914-1918--Juvenile literature. 2. World War, 1914-1918--Campaigns--Juvenile literature. I. Title.

D522.7.G69 2014
940.4--dc23

2014017859

Crabtree Publishing Company

www.crabtreebooks.com   1-800-387-7650

Printed in Canada/052014/MA20140505

Published in Canada
Crabtree Publishing
616 Welland Ave.
St. Catharines, Ontario
L2M 5V6

Published in the United States
Crabtree Publishing
PMB 59051
350 Fifth Avenue, 59th Floor
New York, New York 10118

Published in the United Kingdom
Crabtree Publishing
Maritime House
Basin Road North, Hove
BN41 1WR

Published in Australia
Crabtree Publishing
3 Charles Street
Coburg North
VIC, 3058

CONTENTS

ASSASSINATION TO WAR

When Archduke Franz Ferdinand of Austria was murdered on June 28, 1914, Europe was at peace. His death started a chain reaction leading to what was then called the Great War. It was a war that eventually involved dozens of countries around the world.

The Archduke was heir to the throne of Austria-Hungary, an empire that ruled many nations. The people in these nations came from different ethnic groups and cultures. Serbia, one of those countries, wanted to be independent. A Bosnian-Serb killed Franz Ferdinand as a protest against Austria. Austria wanted to punish Serbia.

Many people believed the tragedy would not have to lead to a war between Austria and Serbia. Unfortunately, Austria was looking for an excuse to start a war. It wanted to **defeat** Serbia and gain territory in Eastern Europe.

Austria's **ally**, Germany, also wanted an excuse to expand its power in Europe. Germany had agreed to support Austria-Hungary if there was a war. In the meantime, Russia had agreed to help Serbia. Few people thought there would actually be a war. If there was one, most believed it would be over in weeks.

The Austrians sent a list of demands to Serbia. Serbia agreed to many of the demands, but Austria was still not satisfied. On July 28, Austria-Hungary declared war on Serbia. The next day, Russia began to **mobilize** troops and

ABOVE: *World War I British recruitment poster*

prepare for war. Germany mobilized in response, and it declared war against Russia on August 1.

France was an ally of Russia. It had to decide whether to support Russia or to not take sides and stay **neutral**. France decided to prepare for war with Germany. The British held back. They were allies with France but hoped that the situation would not escalate.

Germany hoped to quickly defeat France, then send troops to fight against Russia's huge army. The Germans attacked France through Belgium, which was neutral. On August 4, Germany moved into Belgium. Britain, which was allied with Belgium, then declared war on Germany.

Now all of the five major powers in Europe were at war with each other. The Allies—France, Russia, and Britain—were fighting the Central Powers—Germany and Austria-Hungary. The colonies of each empire were drawn into the war as well, sending troops and supplies to the fight in Europe and other places around the world. Each side thought it would quickly win the war and its soldiers would be home by the end of the year.

In cities, citizens were excited by the thought of war. People were swept up in patriotic fever and many young men signed up to fight.

Little did they know that the glorious war they imagined would soon become a nightmare. Instead of going home within months, men found themselves bogged down in muddy trenches for years. They faced enemies across fields of barbed wire and dead or wounded soldiers. In the first two years, from 1914 to 1916, **deadlocked** armies spent month after month in battle. There were few clear victories and millions of **casualties**. The march toward death and destruction had begun.

LEFT: *This painting by British artist John Nash entitled* Over the Top *commemorates the fighting near Cambrai, where British soldiers suffered heavy losses.*

Allied (Entente) Powers

Central Powers

Neutral Powers

Major battlefronts

Italy aligned with Germany in 1914 but joined the war on the Allied side in 1915

Norway

Sweden

Denmark

NORTH SEA

Great Britain

Netherlands

London

Berlin

German Empire

ATLANTIC OCEAN

Belgium

Luxembourg

Paris

WESTERN FRONT

France

Switzerland

ITALIAN FRONT

Montenegro

Italy

Portugal

Corsica

Spain

Sardinia

Sicily

Spanish Morocco

Tunisia

Morocco

Algeria

0   800 miles

0   800 km

Libya

STERN FRONT

Moscow

Russian Empire

CASPIAN SEA

stro-Hungarian Empire

Romanian Campaign

Romania

BLACK SEA

Caucasus Campaign

Serbia

Bulgaria

Balkan Campaign

Constantinople

ania

Dardanelles Campaign

Ottoman Empire

Persia

Mesopotamian Campaign

Greece

Palestinian Campaign

Cyprus

MEDITERRANEAN SEA

Arabia

Egypt

CHAPTER 1

WAR ON THE WESTERN FRONT

Major Events

1914

June 28
A Bosnian-Serb assassinates Archduke Franz-Ferdinand of Austria and his wife Sophie.

July 28
Austria-Hungary declares war on Serbia.

August 1
Germany declares war on Russia.

August 3
Germany declares war on France and prepares to invade Belgium.

August 4
Britain declares war on Germany and Austria-Hungary.

August 6
Battle of the Frontiers begins in Alsace-Lorraine.

August 7
British troops arrive in France.

August 23
Battle of Mons

September 6–12
First Battle of the Marne

1915

April 22–May 25
Second Battle of Ypres; first successful use of poison gas

1916

February 21–December 18
Battle of Verdun

July 1–November 18
Battle of the Somme

Once war was declared, troops from the Allied and Central Powers quickly went into action. Both sides thought they had the **advantage**. The fighting on the Western Front soon became a **stalemate**. Neither side was able to advance very far. Battles were fought from trenches, especially on the Western Front, with a bloody "No Man's Land" in between.

WORLD WAR I BEGINS

A war against France and Russia meant that Germany had to fight on two **fronts**. They fought France on the Western Front. The war with Russia took place on the Eastern Front. Germany had to divide its forces to fight in two places at once.

BELOW: *Troops advanced to the battlefront on foot and on horse.*

The Schlieffen Plan

Germany had a plan of attack called the Schlieffen Plan. This **strategy** called for Germany to strike hard and fast against France. Once Germany won the war there, it could shift its army to the east to fight against Russia.

On August 3, 1914, a massive German army swept into Belgium. The Germans thought that they could surprise France by attacking from the north and quickly advance toward Paris. France and Britain declared war on Germany in response.

The Invasion of Belgium

Germany had a total of 1.5 million troops ready to move into Belgium. Belgium's army had only about 117,000 men. The army was not well trained, and even their uniforms were old. The Germans did not expect much of a fight, but they were wrong.

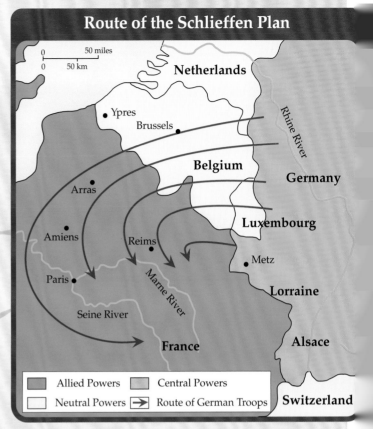

Route of the Schlieffen Plan

Netherlands
Ypres
Brussels
Belgium
Rhine River
Germany
Arras
Luxembourg
Amiens
Reims
Metz
Paris
Marne River
Lorraine
Seine River
France
Alsace
Switzerland

Allied Powers   Central Powers
Neutral Powers   → Route of German Troops

WHAT DO YOU KNOW?

HOWITZERS

The **howitzer** was a new weapon that was developed shortly before the war began. Both sides used this type of heavy **artillery**. Its large shells caused terrible destruction and many deaths. Since they were fired from long distances, howitzers were used to smash enemy fortifications before troops attacked on foot.

The howitzers used to attack the forts of Liège and Namur were made by German and Austrian companies. The German gun was 16.5 in (420 mm)—so large that it could only be moved by train. The smaller Skoda model was 12 in (305 mm) and was carried by vehicles on roads.

The Belgians Fight Back

The cities of Liège and Namur were part of an area that had twelve strong forts. When the Germans attacked, the Belgians defended themselves with deadly machine gun fire, pushing the Germans back. The Germans responded by bringing in giant howitzer guns. The large shells smashed through the Belgian fortifications. Within two weeks, the Germans had captured all the forts and taken the capital of Brussels.

Despite the speed of the German advance, the Belgian army managed to avoid being captured and wiped out. Still, little stood against the Germans as they turned south toward the cities of Charleroi and Namur.

The Belgians had retreated north to Antwerp. The German First and Second Armies approached the French-Belgian border with only an over-extended French Fifth Army and five infantry divisions from the British Expeditionary Force standing in their way.

Germany's Brutal March

The Germans wanted to frighten the Belgians so that they would stop fighting back. They destroyed towns and arrested or killed thousands of Belgian citizens, including children. When news of these **atrocities** got back to the Allied countries and the United States, people were horrified. The world turned against Germany.

BELOW: *Homeless Belgian refugees tried to escape the fighting.*

THE GERMANS ADVANCE INTO FRANCE

The French expected Germany to attack in the south, where they shared a border. That area was called Alsace-Lorraine, which France had lost in the Franco-Prussian War in 1870–1871. The French started their attack there against a smaller German army. The main German force was in the north, with fewer French troops to stop them. The war, however, did not go according to Germany's careful military planning.

Battles of the Frontiers

Under General Joseph Joffre, the French attacked along the Alsace-Lorraine border. However, three German armies, made up of 565,000 men, were ready. There were many fierce battles from August 6 to 21, including combat at Mulhouse, Lorraine, Ardennes, and Charleroi. France, though, made few gains and had terrible losses. Soon it became clear that the Germans' unstoppable march through Belgium, under command of Alexander von Kluck, was the greatest threat. General Joffre used trains to quickly move his army north to meet the great German force.

The Battle of Mons

In August, Britain sent 70,000 troops to northern France, commanded by

JOSEPH JOFFRE
(1852–1931)

General Joffre was the commander-in-chief of French forces until 1916. He was known by his troops as Papa Joffre. Joffre was admired for being cool-headed, even during the most difficult times. At the beginning of the war, he made some mistakes. His decisions, though, helped stop the Germans at the Battle of the Marne.

Field Marshal John French. Although this was a small number, these men were experienced soldiers. At first, Joffre thought that the British and Belgian troops were enough to fight the Germans. While he fought in Alsace-Lorraine, he sent only a small French army north.

On August 23, the British had their first battle with the German army. With 160,000 troops, they were greatly **outnumbered** by the Germans, but the British soldiers were excellent **marksmen**. They held off the Germans with rifle fire. Finally, though, Joffre ordered them to **retreat**. Though the British and French were defeated, they had delayed the German advance by one day. They headed to the Marne River, where Joffre was gathering the Allied forces.

ABOVE: *The French commandeered buses and taxis to transport troops to the Marne.*

The First Battle of the Marne

The Germans continued to **advance** toward Paris. Both sides were exhausted from long marches and carrying heavy supplies in the heat.

The Allied and German forces were more closely matched now. Some German troops had been lost in battle. Others stayed behind to defend German positions. More German armies had to be sent to the Eastern Front as well.

The Germans confidently moved toward the Marne River. The Marne was about 30 miles (48 km) from Paris. People fled the French capital; even the government fled the city. On September 5, Joffre ordered his troops to attack the Germans with everything they had. When more soldiers were needed, the Paris commander sent 6,000 men to the front in hundreds of taxis.

In the meantime, the German forces had to fight attacks on all sides. This split the two parts of the German army even farther apart. Allied planes spotted the hole, and British and French troops moved in. This was the first time that airplanes were used to scout an enemy's position.

On September 9, the Germans started to retreat. About two and a half million soldiers took part in the battle, with over 250,000 casualties on each side. After the Battle of the Marne, the war no longer looked as though it would end soon.

STALEMATE ON THE WESTERN FRONT

After losing the Battle of the Marne, the German army retreated to the Aisne River. They began to dig trenches to defend themselves. From there, they could also launch attacks on other areas.

As the war continued, the trench systems grew. Both sides dug deep, zigzagging lines of defense all along the battlefront. Soon neither side could move forward. The war became a stalemate. Yet the battles continued. By the end of November 1914, over 600,000 French, German, British, and Belgian soldiers had been killed or wounded.

The First Battle of Ypres

The German commander General Eric von Falkenhayn decided to wait to capture Paris. He went north again, planning to capture seaports on the English Channel instead. From September, the Allied and German armies both moved toward the coast in a "Race to the Sea." The Belgians kept the Germans from reaching the coast by opening flood gates on the Yser River. This forced German troops back to Ypres. There they fought British, French, Belgian, and Indian troops in a month of brutal combat.

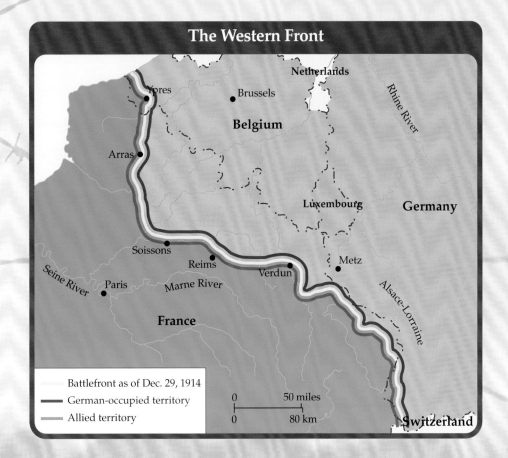

The Western Front

Netherlands

Ypres

Brussels

Rhine River

Belgium

Arras

Luxembourg

Germany

Soissons

Reims

Verdun

Metz

Seine River

Paris

Marne River

Alsace-Lorraine

France

Battlefront as of Dec. 29, 1914
— German-occupied territory
— Allied territory

0   50 miles
0   80 km

Switzerland

The Germans needed more troops to carry out their plans. They **recruited** students who did not have much training. Some were as young as 16. At Ypres, tens of thousands of them were killed. The battle finally ended in the November cold. Many more thousands were dead on both sides. The Germans had been stopped from reaching the English Channel, but there were no clear winners.

> When our guide led me into a trench filled waist deep with muddy water, I could not believe he was serious—and I hesitated—I was wearing brand-new riding-breeches, puttees, and boots. However, I waded in, and it was seventeen days before my boots touched dry soil again.
>
> **FROM B. NEYLAND, A BRITISH RADIO OPERATOR**

RIGHT: Men called stretcher bearers were in charge of carrying wounded or sick soldiers to aid posts to receive medical attention.

Digging In: Trench Warfare

After the First Battle of Ypres, there were 350 miles of trenches along the front. They stretched from the English Channel to the Swiss border. For the rest of the war, the trenches and the front lines hardly moved more than a few hundred yards. The biggest shift was 10 mi (16 km).

Trench Systems Trenches were designed to be deep enough to protect a standing man from artillery shells and gunfire. They often had underground shelters. Machine guns were located near the front lines. Heavy artillery was behind the trenches.

Life in the Trenches The trenches were miserable places that were often muddy and wet. It was very hard to sleep. Many soldiers suffered from painful conditions such as trench foot, which they got from wearing wet boots for days. Rats and lice invaded clothing and spread dangerous diseases.

No Man's Land Between the trenches of the two armies was "No Man's Land." This frightful area was protected by thick stretches of barbed wire and sometimes mine fields. Artillery shells blasted large holes in the ground. The area might be no more than 90 feet (27 m) wide and was seldom longer than a half mile (0.8 km). At night, men went out to bury the dead and clear paths in the barbed wire for another attack in the morning.

A NEW WEAPON

Throughout 1915, the stalemate continued. Joffre ordered an **offensive** in the Champagne region that lasted from December 20, 1914, to March 17, 1915. Though many attacks and **counterattacks** took place, usually very little ground was gained. The number of casualties kept increasing.

The Second Battle of Ypres
By April 1915, the Germans had moved a lot of troops to the Eastern Front. They needed a victory to hide this

RIGHT: *Soldiers choked on the gas, and many were blinded by it.*

WHAT DO YOU THINK?
How did new weapons in World War I change the way wars were fought?

weakness. General Falkenhayn decided to use a new weapon. On April 22, a greenish cloud of gas drifted toward the French trenches. Men started coughing and turning blue from breathing the chlorine gas. Thousands ran to the rear of the trenches. Others lay on the ground choking.

ABOVE: *Gas was a feared weapon that could leave countless soldiers suffering in pain or dead.*

The Germans advanced cautiously. They did not want to catch up to the cloud of gas. Meanwhile, Canadian troops held their position, even though some gas had drifted their way. They found that they could stop the effects of the gas by tying wet cloths over their mouths. The Germans attacked the Canadians with gas again, but the Allied force was able to stop the advance. This was the first time gas was used on the Western Front.

WHAT DO YOU KNOW?

GAS WARFARE

After Ypres, new types of poison gas were used by both sides. Both chlorine and phosgene caused death by choking. Mustard gas burned the skin and caused temporary blindness. If it was inhaled, death could be long and painful.

Depending on the wind conditions, gas could drift back toward the army that used it. Gas masks were quickly developed to protect soldiers. Even though gas did not kill nearly as many men as other weapons, it still caused terrible injuries. After the war, most countries signed a treaty to stop the use of this terrible weapon.

A Joint Action

Joffre knew that the Germans had lost troops that were sent to fight the Russians. In September 1915, Joffre decided to try another offensive in the Champagne region. On September 25, French and British armies launched a series of attacks all along the front. The British also used chlorine gas against the Germans for the first time. The breeze was not right to carry the gas, however, and the effect was limited.

The Germans were well prepared for the attack. Allied troops got past Germany's first line of defense. But thousands of soldiers were cut down by machine-gun fire before they could reach the second line. The assault was thrown back. The Allies needed to come up with new battle **tactics**.

THE BIG PUSH

By the end of 1915, the war had turned into a defensive war. Great Britain sent more troops and weapons to France. Meanwhile, the Germans knew that they were quickly being outnumbered. Both sides felt that they could no longer stay defensive.

The Battle of Verdun

The Allies planned to attack near the Somme River in the summer of 1916. The Germans, however, were planning an

ABOVE: *Soldiers wore gas masks to help protect themselves.*

attack too, before the Allied armies grew too big. Germany was fighting Russia and Italy now. The British navy was also blocking food and supplies from reaching Germany.

France had already lost over 2 million men. General Falkenhayn hoped one big push would finish off the French army. He decided to start his attack on Verdun.

On the morning of February 21, the Germans fired 100,000 shells an hour on French troops. In the afternoon, they started a ground attack. Even though the French were greatly outnumbered and not well prepared, they fought bravely and held their ground.

The battle became a matter of honor for France. In March, three quarters of the French army arrived in Verdun. The Germans threw everything they had at them. Massive attacks and counterattacks continued. With the British attack along the Somme in June, and attacks on the Eastern and Italian Fronts, Germany was stretched thin. By November, new French **offensives** had regained all the territory lost at Verdun.

The Germans had failed, but the French could not celebrate a victory either. Verdun and the villages around it had been destroyed. Half a million men had been killed or wounded. The commanders on both sides, General Falkenhayn and General Joffre, were replaced soon afterward.

> They were direct from the line and their faces were white and drawn and their eyes glassy from lack of sleep. There were great husky men, crying with the pain of gaping wounds and dreadfully discolored trench feet. There were strings of from eight to twenty blind boys filing up the road, their hands on each other's shoulders and their leader some bedraggled, bandaged, limping youngster.
>
> SISTER HELEN DORE BOYLSTON A NURSE, DESCRIBING THE WOUNDED

BELOW: *French soldiers fire grenades from inside a trench during the Battle of Verdun.*

The Battle of the Somme

With the French fighting at Verdun, the British took the main role in the Somme campaign. With over a million men from England, Canada, Australia, New Zealand, India, and South Africa, and careful planning, General Douglas Haig believed it would be a quick battle.

On June 24, the British began shelling German positions. In the next seven days, they fired over one and a half million shells. They thought that the artillery would destroy the trenches and barbed wire. British troops could then easily march across No Man's Land and past the empty front trenches.

Unfortunately, the battle did not go according to Haig's plan. On July 1, the shelling ended. British troops marched forward in long lines, carrying heavy packs. But the shelling had not destroyed German defenses. It only drove the Germans into their deep bunkers.

When the German gunners came out, the British were easy targets. Machine guns mowed them down by the thousands. Over 100,000 men went into battle that day. More than 20,000 were killed and 40,000 wounded. It was the bloodiest day of fighting in British military history.

For the next four months, the two armies continued to fight with no clear winner. Finally, the Allies ended the offensive on November 19. The weather made continuing impossible. Although the Allies had advanced 7 mi (11 km), there were no winners.

ABOVE: *A British Mark I tank, Battle of the Somme*

WHAT DO YOU KNOW?

MARK I TANKS

The Somme was the first battle to use tanks. The British Mark I terrified the Germans at first. It was protected by armor and armed with large naval guns and machine guns. The caterpillar treads could cross barbed wire and climb through trenches. At first, the tanks looked unstoppable and helped the British gain some ground. However, the tanks often broke down or got stuck in mud or ditches. The Germans also found ways of stopping the tanks using artillery or well-placed hand grenades.

CHAPTER 2

WAR ON THE EASTERN FRONT

Major Events

1914

July 28
Austria-Hungary declares war on Serbia.

July 31
Russia mobilizes troops to support Serbia.

August 1
Germany declares war on Russia.

August 6
Austria-Hungary declares war on Russia.

August 17
The first Russian forces cross into Germany.

August 18
Russia invades Galicia (part of Poland under Austro-Hungarian rule).

August 26
The Battle of Tannenberg begins.

1915

May 2
The Battle of Gorlice-Tarnow begins.

July 22
The Russians pull out of Poland.

1916

June 4
Brusilov Offensive begins.

The Eastern Front ran along the borders of Germany, Russia, and Austria-Hungary. The Eastern Front was so long, trench warfare was not used as much. The Allies wanted to force Germany to send troops to the Eastern Front. That way, the Germans would have fewer troops to fight on the Western Front in France. Russia agreed to launch a massive attack soon after war was declared.

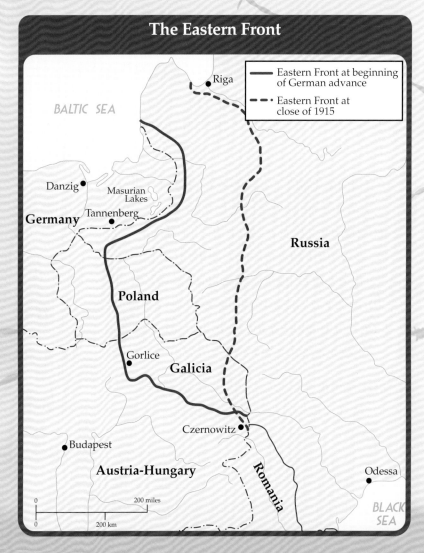

The Eastern Front

Eastern Front at beginning of German advance

Eastern Front at close of 1915

Riga

BALTIC SEA

Danzig
Masurian Lakes
Tannenberg

Germany

Russia

Poland

Gorlice

Galicia

Czernowitz

Budapest

Austria-Hungary

Romania

Odessa

BLACK SEA

0   200 miles

0   200 km

RUSSIA ATTACKS

The Central Powers thought that Russia would take a long time to mobilize. The Russians, though, wanted to strike fast. They knew the German armies on the Eastern Front were weak.

Russian forces outnumbered the Germans almost three to one. However, the Russians were not as prepared as the Germans. Many of the soldiers did not have rifles or even boots. Poor roads and rail connections made it difficult to get supplies. Many commanders were unskilled.

Russia Attacks Germany

Russia decided to attack the eastern part of Germany with two armies. These armies circled around the German army, either destroying it or making it retreat. After that, the Russians joined together and continued toward the German capital of Berlin. On August 17, 1914, the first army under General Pavel Rennenkampf crossed the border. A few days later, the second army moved in from the south, commanded by General Alexander Samsonov.

At first, Russian forces drove the Germans back. However, the two Russian armies were now about 50 mi (80.5 km) apart—separated by the Masurian Lakes region. They could not easily support or communicate with each other.

WHAT DO YOU THINK?
How did Russia's attacks on the Eastern Front affect the battles on the Western Front?

The Germans Strike Back

The Germans brought in two experienced commanders to lead them on the Eastern Front: Generals Paul von Hindenburg and Erich Ludendorff. The German commanders decided to attack one Russian army at a time. They moved most of their troops into position to meet Samsonov's southern army, which they now outnumbered.

BELOW: *Many Russian soldiers attacked the Germans on horseback during the Battle of Tannenberg.*

The Battle of Tannenberg

On August 26, the German and Russian forces met. By August 29, the Germans had destroyed much of Samsonov's army. Russian soldiers ran for their lives. Ninety thousand men were taken prisoner. Samsonov felt very guilty about that and killed himself.

Meanwhile, Rennenkampf's army did not know what had happened. They didn't realize that the Germans had only left a weak army to fight them. By then, though, the Germans had sent troops from the Western Front.

The First Battle of the Masurian Lakes

The Germans now outnumbered Rennenkampf's army. From September 7–13, both sides fought fiercely, but the Germans forced the Russians back to their border. Although the Germans suffered great losses, the Russians had more. Almost 100,000 men were killed or wounded and another 45,000 were taken prisoner.

BELOW: *The Austro–Hungarian army fights off the Russians at Bukovina.*

INVASIONS OF POLAND AND GALICIA

The victories at Tannenberg and the Masurian Lakes had given Germany more confidence. They had also shaken the Allies' confidence in Russia. Fortunately, Russia had more success against Austria-Hungary.

Poland was part of Russia during World War I. The Russians started building up their troops along the border of Galicia, which was ruled by Austria-Hungary. Austria attacked Poland on August 25, 1914. By September, the Austrian army was defeated. The loss was so terrible that the Austrian army never recovered completely. The Russians had also lost hundreds of thousands of men. However, they had taken most of Galicia.

At the end of September, Germany sent troops to help Austria-Hungary in Poland. The Germans got almost as far as Warsaw, Poland's capital. However, they had to withdraw due to supply problems, exhaustion, and too few men.

Bloody battles continued in Poland through 1914. The Russians lost the city of Lodz to Germany but were able to hold their position around Warsaw. By then it was clear that Austria-Hungary could not survive without the help of Germany. Losses on both sides were in the millions. Russia, though, could still find men for its armies, while Austria could not.

THE BATTLES OF 1915

In 1915, Germany's kaiser ordered his commanders to send more troops to the Eastern Front. The Germans weren't sure whether to attack in the north or the south. They decided to do both.

Northern Attacks

Russia was preparing to cross into German territory once again. To distract Russia, Germany attacked Bolimov, a city near Warsaw, Poland. Bolimov was the first battle where a large-scale gas attack was used in World War I. But it was January, so most of the gas froze before it was released in the air.

A few weeks later, Germany attacked the Russians again at the Masurian Lakes. The fierce battle began during a snowstorm on February 8, 1915. After two weeks of ferocious fighting, the Russians surrendered. The next day, another Russian army counterattacked and stopped Germany's advance

BELOW: *Russian soldiers march through the snow to battle.*

toward Warsaw. This convinced the Germans to combine forces with Austria and to focus on the Galicia region to the south.

Germany Moves Forward

The Austrians were having trouble in Galicia. The winter weather and poor roads made it hard for them to advance. The fighting went back and forth. At the end of April, the Austrians stopped the Russian advance.

In the spring, more German units were brought in from the Western Front. On May 2, they launched a ferocious attack. Without artillery support, the Russians were forced back. The Germans continued to push north from Galicia. In two months, they took back all the territory that Russia had captured in 1914.

The Germans continued to advance through the summer and into the fall. Russian armies were short of weapons and supplies. They gave up 300 mi (483 km) of territory.

THE BRUSILOV OFFENSIVE

Fighting was lighter during Russia's cold winter. The Germans were focused on the brutal battles in Verdun. In March, the French asked Russia to launch an attack. They wanted Germany to send more troops to the Eastern Front to reduce its force in Verdun. The Russians agreed, but they were defeated by the Germans. The Russians looked weak to the Allies. The war was also losing the support of the Russian people.

Italy asked Russia for help against Austria-Hungary. Russia sent troops led by General Alexei Brusilov. Brusilov came up with a new strategy to confuse the Central Powers. Russian armies would strike at different places. That way Germany and Austria couldn't tell where the main target of the attack would be.

Brusilov prepared by stocking up on weapons and moving trenches closer to the Austrian front line. He used photos taken by airplanes to see where the Germans had their guns. He even made models of Austrian defenses so his men could train in them.

ALEXEI BRUSILOV
(1853–1926)

General Alexei Brusilov came from a long line of officers who had served in the czar's armies. He joined a military academy when he was 14. By the time he was 24, he was a lieutenant. He was a skilled horseman. In 1912, he became the general of **cavalry**.

During World War I, Brusilov proved himself to be one of Russia's best commanders. His intelligence and strength helped him convince Russian leaders to follow his offensive plan. Even his enemies admired and copied his military strategies. After the Russian Revolution, he was appointed minister of war in the new government.

RIGHT: *Russian infantry advanced during the Brusilov offensive on the Eastern Front.*

The Russians caught the enemy by surprise on June 4. Brusilov's strategies worked as he had planned. By June 23, Russian forces had forced the Austrians to flee from their front lines. Alarmed, the Germans sent more troops to help Austria-Hungary.

Brusilov expected help from Russian General Alexei Evert. Evert was supposed to attack the Germans on June 14, but he refused to move until July 3. Evert's hesitation ruined Brusilov's plans. Despite his great success, he had to end his offensive in September.

Brusilov had not achieved everything he wanted, but he almost destroyed Austria-Hungary's army. He also helped the Italians and the French by drawing away Austrian and German troops. However, Russia lost almost one and a half million men—over twice as many men as the Austrians. The Russian people saw it as another failure.

> [The Austrians] started a desperate assault during the early hours of the 25th of August.... For a whole day they fought without intermission, and thousands of men perished in trenches that had to be carried with the bayonet. The Russians retired towards the Bug [River], defending their ground inch by inch, burning the town, blowing up the railway station, the post-office (buildings that might prove of some utility [use] to the enemy), and the barracks which had been occupied by their troops.
>
> PRINCESS CATHERINE RADZIWILL, DESCRIBING THE FALL OF THE FORTRESS TOWN OF KOVNO

ABOVE: *Among the 1.4 million Russian soliders lost during the Brusilov Offensive, over 210,000 were taken as prisoners of war.*

CHAPTER 3

WAR ON THE BALKAN FRONT

Major Events

1914

June 28
A Bosnian-Serb assassinates Archduke Franz Ferdinand of Austria and his wife Sophie

July 28
Austria-Hungary declares war on Serbia.

July 29
Austria begins to shell Serbia. Russia, Serbia's ally, mobilizes its army.

August 12
Austria-Hungary invades Serbia.

October 28
Turkey joins the Central Powers.

1915

September 6
Bulgaria joins the Central Powers.

November 23
Serbia is defeated.

1916

August 27
Romania declares war on Austria-Hungary.

In 1914, the Balkan region was made up of Serbia, Bulgaria, Romania, Montenegro, Albania, and Greece. This area stood between Europe, southern Russia, and the Ottoman Empire in Turkey. When the Ottomans entered the war, they sided with the Central Powers. The Balkans were a key supply route from Germany and Austria to Turkey.

THE INVASION OF SERBIA

On July 28, 1914, as the war began, the Austrians began to fire artillery shells into Belgrade, the capital of Serbia. By August 12, Austria had mobilized its army, which greatly outnumbered the Serbs.

The Balkan Campaign

Austria-Hungary
German army
Austro-Hungarian army
Belgrade
Romania
Bucharest
Serbia
Bulgarian 1st Army
Bulgarian 3rd Army
Montenegro
Cetinje
Sofia
Bulgaria
Bulgarian 2nd Army
Durrës
ADRIATIC SEA
Albania
BLACK SEA
Greece
Ottoman Empire
AEGEAN SEA

⊠ Bulgarian army
⊠ German and A-H armies
⊠ Serbian army
→ Central forces movement
⊠ Allied forces movement

0   150 miles
0   150 km

The Austrians planned to capture Belgrade and other key cities before Serbian troops were ready to fight.

Austria had to send an army north to stop the Russians in Galicia. Even with less manpower, the Austrians were confident. In August and September, though, Austria lost battle after battle to the tough Serbs.

The Serbs were soon short on supplies and ammunition. On December 1, Austria finally captured Belgrade but found it deserted. The government and the army had moved to another city.

Even though Austria had taken important cities, they could not defeat the Serbian armies. The French sent the Serbs more ammunition and the fighting continued. By mid-December, the Serbs retook Belgrade. By the end of the year, they had regained all of Serbia and even some Austrian territory.

BULGARIA ENTERS THE WAR

When the Central Powers lost Serbia, Bulgaria became more important as a potential ally. On September 6, 1915, Bulgaria allied itself with Germany and Austria-Hungary. In return, the Central

> "… the rain, which churned up the mud, and soaked the ill-clad people, was called by the Serbians 'the little friend of Serbia,' for it held up the Austrian advance, and consequently saved practically the whole of Serbia's remaining Army."
>
> **ACCOUNT BY A BRITISH NURSE SERVING IN SERBIA**

Powers promised to give Bulgaria land in Serbia and northern Greece.

When Bulgaria entered the war, Britain and France were not immediately able to send troops to help Serbia. The Central Powers did not wait. Germany and Austria-Hungary invaded Serbia from the north on October 6. Five days later, Bulgaria sent in an army from the south. By late November, Serbia had lost most of its territory.

BELOW: *Bulgarian troops arm their trench with guns facing Serbia.*

The Serbian government, army, and **civilian** refugees retreated to Albania. Starving and sick people crossed freezing, icy mountains. They reached the city of Shkodër, only to face air strikes from Austrian planes. At last, Allied ships helped them reach the island of Corfu in Greece. The Central Powers were now in control of Serbia, as well as Albania and Montenegro.

ROMANIA JOINS THE ALLIES

The Danube River runs along the border of Romania and Bulgaria to the Black Sea. Romania could control this important route for transporting goods through the Balkans. Romania was important to the Central Powers and the Allies. The Allies promised Romania that they could have the territory of Transylvania in Austria-Hungary. On August 27, 1916, Romania declared war on Austria-Hungary.

Unfortunately, the Romanians had a poorly trained army. They had old equipment, and the Allies did not send the supplies and weapons they needed. At first, the Romanian army had some success, capturing part of Transylvania.

WHAT DO YOU THINK?
Why were the Balkans so important to both the Central Powers and the Allies?

Germany, however, came to the aid of Austria. German, Bulgarian, and Turkish troops pushed back the Romanians. On October 23, Romania's main port on the Black Sea fell. By the middle of November, the Germans had taken back Transylvania and invaded Romania. The Romanians bravely defended their country, but the capital of Bucharest fell on December 6.

RIGHT: *Germany brought troops across the Danube River to fight the Romanians.*

28

CHAPTER 4

WAR AT SEA

Britain and Germany relied on shipping to get food and supplies for their countries. These supplies were critical for feeding their people and waging a war.

In 1914, Great Britain's Home Fleet was the largest navy in the world. Germany's High Seas Fleet, though smaller, was still a great threat. Each nation had plans to stop important supply shipments from reaching the other. Britain decided to **blockade** German ports and shipping routes. Germany used its U-boats, or submarines, to stop ships traveling to England.

Major Events

1914

August 28
First naval battle at
Heligoland Bight

November 3
Britain begins naval blockade
of Germany.

1915

February 18
Germany starts unrestricted
warfare against enemy vessels.

May 7
Lusitania is sunk
by a German U-boat.

1916

May 31
Battle of Jutland

The War in the North Sea

0 — 300 miles
0 — 300 km

ATLANTIC OCEAN

Shetland Islands

Scapa Flow

Orkney Islands

Scotland

Norway

Battle of Jutland

NORTH SEA

Ireland

IRISH SEA

Dublin

Wales

England

Heligoland

London

Amsterdam

Hamburg

Dover

Netherlands

ENGLISH CHANNEL

Calais

Antwerp

Belgium

Germany

Paris

France

Northern patrol and mines

Naval war zone declared by Germany in 1915

Dover patrol and mines

ENGLAND CLEARS THE SEAS

A few weeks after the war started, the British sent ships and submarines to the island of Heligoland in the North Sea. The German fleet there guarded an important shipping route between the North Sea and the Baltic Sea. The British attack surprised the Germans. Seven German warships were sunk or damaged. Only three British vessels were badly damaged.

ABOVE: *Heavily armed British battleships played a major role in the war.*

Battle of the Falklands

On November 1, 1914, German Admiral Maximilian Graf von Spee attacked four British warships off the coast of Chile. Two British ships were sunk, and the other two escaped.

The British were shocked at this loss. They were also worried that the Germans would attack other naval bases in the area. They sent a squadron of eight ships to the Falkland Islands off the coast of Argentina. Admiral Spee did not know that British warships had arrived at the Falklands. He was not prepared for them when he tried to attack. Spee quickly fled when he saw what he was up against, but the British soon caught up with him. All but one of the German ships were sunk. The British suffered light damage. This was the last action of the German navy in the Atlantic.

KARL VON MÜLLER
(1873–1923)

The British and German navies sent ships far from their countries. German Captain Karl von Müller and his ship SMS *Emden* were especially successful. Even his enemies admired his heroism and daring. Müller cruised the Pacific and Indian Oceans from the German port in Tsingtao, China. He destroyed many Allied warships and trade vessels. Finally, in November 1914, the SMS *Emden* was destroyed by an Australian ship. Müller and his men escaped and returned home to a hero's welcome.

Blockade of Germany

The British navy captured many German merchant ships or forced them to neutral ports. By November, Britain had started a naval blockade against Germany. It declared the North Sea a war zone. Ships from any country could be stopped and searched. If the British found any goods being sent to Germany, they took them.

THE GERMAN SUBMARINE BLOCKADE

The Germans began submarine attacks soon after the war started. On September 22, a German U-boat sank three British cruisers in the English Channel, killing 1,500 sailors. In January 1915, the Germans lost a naval battle at Dogger Bank in the North Sea. With the British blockade on, Germany did not want to risk losing more large ships. It decided to expand the use of U-boats instead.

Unrestricted Warfare

In February 1915, Germany declared that the seas around Britain were a war zone. That meant that they might attack any vessel there without warning. This included neutral merchant ships that might be carrying war supplies to the Allies. U-boats torpedoed ships without considering the safety of those aboard. The Germans warned neutral countries that citizens traveling to war zones were in danger.

ABOVE: *A defeated German U-boat on a British beach*

WHAT DO YOU KNOW?

U-BOATS

U-boats is short for the German word *Unterseebooten*, which means "undersea boats." Britain and other nations had submarines, but none used them as a major weapon, like the Germans did.

Germany built its first U-boat in 1903. By the end of the war, Germany had a fleet of 390. U-boats were slow and could only stay underwater a few hours. However, the torpedoes they launched were deadly to ships. It wasn't until 1917 that Britain developed ways to defend its vessels against U-boat attacks.

The U.S. Gets Involved

Germany's actions risked bringing the neutral United States into the war. President Woodrow Wilson made it clear that American citizens had the right to trade with and travel to any warring nation. The Germans agreed to stop the U-boat attacks if Britain stopped its blockade of food and raw materials. Britain was willing to allow food to be shipped to Germany. However, it did not want to allow raw materials that could be used for war goods. The British continued their blockade.

The *Lusitania*

The *Lusitania* was a British luxury liner—one of the largest and fastest passenger ships to sail the Atlantic. On May 1, 1915, it sailed for England from New York. The Germans placed an ad in the newspapers saying that passengers sailed at their own risk. Still, many people didn't believe that U-boats would target a passenger ship.

On May 7, the *Lusitania* was close to England. Passengers suddenly heard an explosion as a German torpedo smashed into the ship. Water poured in, and the ship tilted sharply. In just 15 minutes, the *Lusitania* sank. There had been almost 2,000 passengers on board. Of those, 1,200 drowned, including 128 Americans.

ABOVE: *Sinking of the British luxury liner* Lusitania, *May 7, 1915*

The American public was horrified. Germans defended themselves by saying that the ship carried a load of ammunition bound for England. Many Americans, though, called for war with Germany.

While President Wilson was determined to stay neutral, the Germans were still worried that their actions could draw the United States into the war. They agreed to warn vessels before they attacked. U-boat captains were ordered not to sink passenger ships.

This policy changed a number of times over the next year. Germany continued to torpedo merchant ships. In March 1916, a U-boat sank the *Sussex*, a French passenger ship. These actions continued to turn America against Germany.

THE BATTLE OF JUTLAND

The naval blockades made life difficult in many countries. People had to **ration** food because of shortages. Despite U-boat attacks, British boats were able to bring in enough food for the first three years of the war. The Germans, however, were starving.

It was no longer enough to send submarines to sink British ships. The German naval commander, Admiral Reinhard Scheer, decided he had to defeat the British navy once and for all. On May 31, 1916, his fleet moved into the North Sea to challenge the British. The British Grand Fleet sailed from Scotland to meet them.

The two fleets combined had over 250 ships.

They met off the coast of Denmark, near Jutland. Both sides opened fire. Within hours, the large guns caused major damage to both navies. Three British cruisers went down with all their men after being hit. The British, though, had more fire power and forced the German fleet to turn back.

By the next morning, the biggest sea battle of the war was over. There were no clear winners. Britain had lost more men and ships, but Germany did not have enough ships to return to battle. There were a few smaller naval battles after that, but German warships stayed mostly in their home ports. The British blockade continued, and Germany stepped up its U-boat attacks.

BELOW: *The Battle of Jutland*

WAR ARTISTS

World War I was the subject of many artworks. Some were created by artists who fought in the war. Others were created from the imaginations of artists. Some artists showed very realistic scenes of battles and soldiers. Others tried to portray the horrors in **abstract** ways. Abstract paintings expressed the emotion rather than specific details of events.

Art as Propaganda

Propaganda is information that helps a government. It usually appeals to people's emotions. Governments wanted their citizens to see war images that made it look like their own country was winning. They needed their people to support the war. They wanted to convince men to **enlist**.

The governments of some countries hired **official** artists to paint scenes of the war. The pictures were put in magazines so citizens could see the heroic deeds of their soldiers. The artists were told not to show dead men or images that would upset people. Many artists were unhappy that they could not show the terrible scenes that they witnessed.

Paul Nash, a British war artist complained, "I am no longer an artist interested and curious, I am a messenger who will bring back word from the men who are fighting to those who want the war to go on for ever. Feeble, inarticulate will be my message, but it will have a bitter truth, and may it burn their lousy souls."

RIGHT: *Painting by war artist Paul Nash entitled* Spring in the Trenches, Ridge Wood, 1917

ABOVE: *This George Leroux painting entitled* L'Enfer (Hell) *gives a vivid image of the reality of war.*

War as Art

Many official artists still created powerful images of war's destruction. Ruined buildings and discarded objects often stood in for human suffering. A.Y. Jackson was one of the Canadian artists in the Group of Seven. He served as a war artist after he was wounded early in the war.

John Nash, Paul's brother, painted a battle where he was one of the few survivors. His stark image *Over the Top* gets across the fear the soldiers must have felt.

Some artists painted images from their own memories or from quick sketches they drew during the war. The pictures of German artist Otto Dix were drawn from sketches and from memories. They often have a nightmare quality. Dix served as a machine gunner on the Western and Eastern Fronts. Viewers can get a sense of the horror he felt.

Not all World War I artists served in the war. George Bellows, an American, had only read about the terrible tragedies in Belgium. He was so moved that he created a series of five paintings in 1918. His harsh images shocked Americans.

CHAPTER 5

WORLD WAR I AT GALLIPOLI

Turkey guarded the important water passage between the Mediterranean Sea and the Black Sea. The Allies and Central Powers needed that route to send weapons, food, and supplies. When the Ottoman Empire joined the Central Powers, it was a threat to Russia. The Ottomans could cut off critical war goods and attack Russia from the south.

ATTACK BY SEA

By the end of 1914, fighting on the Western Front had become deadlocked. The British thought they could use their strong naval power to end the stalemate elsewhere. Britain believed a victory at sea might drive the Turks out of the war and boost **morale**.

The First Success

The British and French sent ships armed with heavy guns to the Dardanelles. It was guarded by Turkish forts, and artillery had been placed along land strips on both sides. Britain planned to **bombard** these defenses until they fell, clearing the way to Constantinople,

Turkey's capital. The naval commander Admiral Sackville Carden believed that he could finish the job in a month. On February 19, Carden began to shell the forts near the entrance to the Dardanelles. As the ships went farther in, they met greater resistance from the Turkish guns on higher ground. Worse, the attacks made it hard to look for deadly mines in the water.

Major Events

1914

October 29
Turkey joins the Central Powers.

1915

February 19
Allied naval attack on Gallipoli peninsula

April 25
British, French, and ANZAC forces land in Turkey.

August 6
The Allies bring in more troops.

December
Allies start to withdraw troops from Gallipoli.

RIGHT: *Troops from Australia and New Zealand on their way to Gallipoli*

Threats From Above and Below

Carden told the British government that they could not go on. They needed troops to stop the Turkish forces on land. The government did not want to send troops that were already needed on the Western Front. It urged Carden to carry on.

The large fleet of ships continued slowly through the narrow passageway. On March 18, the British ships began a massive attack on the Turkish forts. Within hours, many ships had been damaged or sunk by mines or shells fired from above. A few days later, the British fleet turned back. The British government agreed to send Carden troops to support the battle effort.

INVASION OF GALLIPOLI

When they left, the British didn't realize that the Turkish army had run short of ammunition. The Turks also had few troops ready to fight. By the time the Allied forces returned in April, however, the Turks were prepared for them.

The First Landing

The British had few maps and little information about Turkish forces with which to plan. They decided to attack the

ABOVE: *ANZAC troops landed on the beach at Gallipoli on April 25, 1915.*

peninsula at Gallipoli. The Allied landing force included well-trained British soldiers, French troops, and the new Australian and New Zealand Army Corps (ANZAC). Over 250 ships supported the army. Battleships bombarded the shore as the men landed.

Meanwhile, the Turkish army occupied the rocky hills above the beaches. Some of the landing parties faced brutal machine gun fire by the defending Turks. Others met very little or no fighting.

WHAT DO YOU THINK?
Why were the Dardanelles so well protected?

ANZAC troops tried to take higher ground before the Turks could reach them, but they weren't successful and suffered heavy losses. After a bloody day, the Allies finally gained some ground on the shore.

By May, the fighting reached another stalemate, and both sides had dug in. The Allies, though, still felt they had to win this battle.

The Second Landing

In August, the Allies brought in thousands more troops. Although they landed successfully, there were still many losses. The Turks fought fiercely. The Allies did not know how low the Turks were on manpower and ammunition.

The burning hot summer made the Allies' camps horrible. There was a water shortage, and men were dying of disease and wounds. Often, the Turkish soldiers fired on them from the hills above.

With the fall of Serbia, the Central Powers had a route to supply Turkey more easily. By October, it was clear that the Allies' position would not improve without more men. As the freezing winter settled in, the Allied troops were miserable. The British decided their only choice was to leave the peninsula. On the night of December 18–19, troops began withdrawing. This continued into January.

The invasion of Gallipoli was a costly failure for the Allies. Many men were killed, wounded, or captured. Turkey was still in the war. Crucial supplies could not reach Russia through the Dardanelles.

WHAT DO YOU KNOW?

THE ANZAC FORCES

When Britain went to war, Canada, Australia, and New Zealand immediately supported the action. They all declared war on Germany. Their citizens eagerly signed up to serve.

The Australian and New Zealand Army Corps (ANZAC) was first sent to Egypt for training. At Gallipoli, they were part of a large international force that fought bravely under terrible conditions. ANZAC troops also protected the Suez Canal and fought in the trenches of Europe and on Pacific islands. ANZAC Day is an important Australian and New Zealand holiday celebrated on April 25. It honors the men and women who served in all wars.

BELOW: *ANZAC troops were armed with cannons and heavy artillery in their battle with the Turks.*

WORLD WAR I ON OTHER FRONTS

CHAPTER 6

The Allies and Central Powers needed all the support they could get. They were desperate for troops, supplies, and strategic territory. Neutral neighbors such as Italy were pressured by both sides to join them. Soon, the war spread beyond Europe.

Many European countries had large empires with colonies in Asia, the Middle East, and Africa. These regions supplied many valuable resources, and they were desirable prizes in the war. The people in these distant lands would also be drawn into the conflict.

ITALY JOINS THE ALLIES

Italy was neutral for much of the first year of the war. However, its rulers wanted territory that belonged to Austria-Hungary. On April 26, 1915, the Allies signed a treaty with Italy.

Major Events

1914

August 26
German and British colonies enter the war.

September 2
Japan and Britain attack German ports in China.

1915

May 23
Italy declares war on Austria-Hungary.

June 23
The Battles of the Isonzo begin.

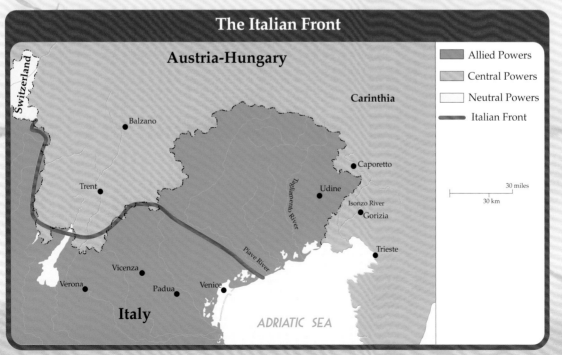

The Italian Front

Switzerland

Austria-Hungary

Carinthia

Balzano

Caporetto

Trent

Udine

Isonzo River

Gorizia

Tagliamento River

Trieste

Vicenza

Piave River

Verona

Padua

Venice

Italy

ADRIATIC SEA

Allied Powers
Central Powers
Neutral Powers
Italian Front

30 miles
30 km

They promised to give Italy land in Europe, Turkey, and even Africa. The Allies hoped that the Italians would draw Austrian troops away from the Eastern Front. Italy declared war against Germany and Austria-Hungary on May 23, 1915.

The Battles of the Isonzo

The Italians chose to attack at the Isonzo River on June 23. This was in a rugged valley at the base of the Alps. The Italians fought four battles at the Isonzo in 1915 but, each time, the Austrians kept them from gaining much ground. Fighting soon resembled the trench warfare on the Western Front. The last of at least 12 battles at the Isonzo was fought in 1917, but the Italians had done little to relieve pressure from Russia.

ABOVE: *Moving men and equipment through the Alps was difficult and treacherous for the Austro-Hungarian army.*

The Italian Front in 1916

In May 1916, Austria-Hungary attacked Italy through the mountains. Moving troops, supplies, and artillery over the Alps was extremely difficult. It gave the Italians time to prepare. The Austrians were turned back by June, and the Italian army continued its offensive on the Isonzo.

This time, Italy's actions drew Austrian troops from Russia's southern front. This allowed Russian General Alexei Brusilov to carry out his offensive.

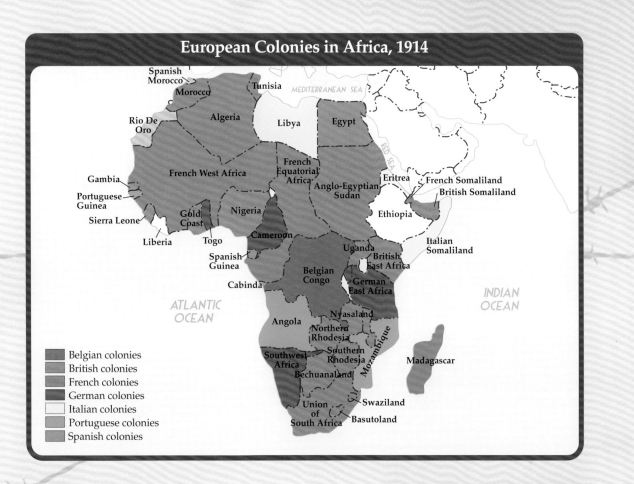

European Colonies in Africa, 1914

Legend:
- Belgian colonies
- British colonies
- French colonies
- German colonies
- Italian colonies
- Portuguese colonies
- Spanish colonies

IMPERIALISM AND WORLD WAR I

Imperialism is when a country wants to rule another country. The country that is taken over is called a **colony**. At the time of the war, colonies were desirable because they often had valuable resources, such as farmland or oil. Or they could be in a strategic location, such as Egypt, where the Suez Canal was built.

Britain had many colonies. India was a colony that supplied many troops who fought for the Allies. Germany wanted to add more colonies to its empire.

QUESTION?
Why did Britain extend the war to the colonies?

During World War I, many nations saw an opportunity to get colonies for themselves.

The Siege of Tsingtao

Germany had a number of colonies in Asia and the Pacific with useful naval ports. Japan wanted to push Germany out of Asia and take its colonies for itself, particularly Tsingtao (now called Qingdao) in China.

ABOVE: *Japanese siege at Tsingtao, China*

Tsingtao had strong defenses, but the German forces there were small with little ammunition. With Britain's help, Japan launched an attack on Tsingtao. Japanese ships blockaded the harbor and pounded the German defenses with artillery. On September 2, troops landed for a ground attack. The Japanese outnumbered the Germans 13 to one. Airplanes supported the attack.

After a fierce fight, the Germans surrendered on November 7. They were out of ammunition. Germany's defeat helped make Japan a major power in the Pacific.

World War I in Africa

German colonies in Africa were surrounded by British and French territories. Britain and Germany needed their troops and resources in Europe. Because of that, it seemed that Africa might stay neutral. Britain, though, wanted to protect its colonies and block Germany's African trade. The Allied nations also wanted Germany's colonies for themselves.

Togoland and Cameroon Britain attacked the tiny German colony of Togoland in August 1914. A radio station in Togoland was used to guide German naval ships. Within weeks, the country was in the hands of the British and French.

Cameroon was larger and took longer to conquer. British and French forces invaded in September 1914. During the wet season, troops battled in pouring rain and carried equipment through swamps. Over time, the British were able to bring in more men and get support from ships on the coast. The Germans finally surrendered in February 1916.

German Southwest Africa Southwest Africa was located next to the Union of South Africa, which was loyal to Britain.

> " The story of War is told in the thousand and one things that mingle with the earth—equipment, bits of clothing almost unrecognizable, an old boot stuck up from a mound of filth, a remnant of sock inside, . . . "
>
> FRED VARLEY, CANADIAN FIRST WORLD WAR ARTIST

South Africa's leader was Louis Botha. When war broke out, Botha had to put down a revolt. Once that had been taken care of, Botha moved his troops into neighboring Southwest Africa, which the Germans controlled. By July, Botha had taken Windhoek, the capital of the colony.

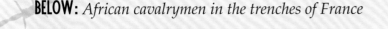

BELOW: *African cavalrymen in the trenches of France*

German East Africa The German commander, Colonel Paul Lettow-Vorbeck, led raids against the British colonies from Germany's colony in East Africa. British forces got help against von Lettow from the South Africans and other allies. By September 1916, Lettow-Vorbeck had lost ground in East Africa, but he successfully continued his campaign in other colonies until the end of the war.

SUMMARY: WORLD WAR I TO THE END OF 1916

When the war began in 1914, the major players were all sure that it would end in months. Instead, all sides found themselves locked in endless battles. There were no clear winners and an unimaginable number of casualties.

Modern weapons changed the way wars were fought. Machine guns and heavy artillery tore through men, causing hundreds of thousands of deaths. Poison gas found those who escaped the shelling. Armies turned to trench warfare and defensive battles, unable to gain any ground.

By 1916, the Great War had turned into a world war. In addition to the Western Front, men were fighting in Eastern Europe, the Balkans, Italy, and Turkey. On the seas, ships were targeted in almost every ocean. People in lands far from Europe were fighting for countries they had never seen.

The war ground to a bloody, costly stalemate. However, in 1917, two major events would change the course of the conflict. One power, Russia, would leave the war, when the people rose up against the czar. Another power, the United States, would finally decide it could no longer remain neutral.

WHAT DO YOU KNOW?

AFRICAN COMBAT

The fighting in Africa looked very different from the battlefronts in Europe. There were no trenches. Troops often moved huge distances despite difficult ground with few roads. Soldiers had to deal with scorching heat, sickness from tsetse flies, and even enemy troops on elephants.

Although officers were white, Allied soldiers were often African or Indian. Black natives were also used to carry supplies and were often treated badly. Africans often had to deal with severe racism.

FURTHER READING AND WEBSITES

BOOKS

Hart, Peter. *The Somme: The Darkest Hour on the Western Front.* New York: Pegasus Books, 2010.

Mayhew, Emily. *Wounded: A New History of the Western Front in World War I.* New York: Oxford University Press, 2014.

Meyer, G.J. *A World Undone: The Story of the Great War, 1914 to 1918.* New York: Delacorte Press, 2007.

Mosier, John. V*erdun: The Lost History of the Most Important Battle of World War I, 1914–1918.* New York: NAL Caliber, 2013.

Prior, Robin. *Gallipoli: The End of the Myth.* New Haven: Yale University Press, 2009.

Remarque, Erich Maria, and A.W. Wheen. *All Quiet on the Western Front.* New York: Fawcett Books, 1987.

Sumner, Ian. *The First Battle of the Marne 1914: The French 'miracle' halts the Germans (Campaign 221).* Oxford: Osprey Publishing, 2010.

Tuchman, Barbara W. *The Guns of August.* New York: Presidio Press, 2004

Willmott, H.P. *World War I.* New York: DK Publishing, 2009.

WEBSITES

The Somme
www.warmuseum.ca/cwm/ exhibitions/guerre/the-somme-e.aspx

The Trenches: Symbol of the Stalemate
www.pbs.org/greatwar/chapters/ ch1_trench.html

The Great War Timeline–1914
www.greatwar.co.uk/timeline/ ww1-events-1914.htm

GLOSSARY

abstract	related to general ideas rather than specific objects or actions
advance	to move or bring forward
advantage	a benefit of something or some event
ally	a country that supports and helps another country during war
artillery	large caliber weapons, such as cannons, that are operated by crews
atrocities	vicious, cruel acts, including the wartime killing of civilians and innocent people
blockade	isolation or blocking a harbor to stop people or supplies from entering or leaving a country
bombard	to attack with bombs, explosive shells, or missiles
casualties	people who are injured or killed during a war or in an accident
cavalry	soldiers who fight on horseback or in light armored vehicles
civilian	a person who is not in the military
colony	a territory that is controlled by or belongs to another country
counterattacks	attacks by a defending force against an attacking enemy force
deadlocked	unable to end a disagreement
defeat	to win victory over; to beat in a contest or in battle
defense	the act of protecting something
enlist	to sign up for service in the armed forces
fronts	areas where military forces are fighting; the most forward lines of a combat force
howitzer	a short cannon that delivers shells at a high trajectory or angle
imperialism	practice of extending a nation's power by gaining control over other nations or territories
marksmen	people who are very skilled at shooting accurately
mobilize	to gather soldiers together and make them ready for action or for war

morale	attitudes of enthusiasm or willingness that a person or a group has about a job
neutral	not aligned with or supporting a side in war, dispute, or contest
offensives	military plans of attack
official	done with or by a person of authority
outnumbered	to be more numerous than
propaganda	ideas, information, or rumors spread for the purpose of helping or hurting an organization, issue, or person
ration	to control the amount that a person can obtain or be given of something such as gasoline or food
recruited	convinced people to join a group or activity, such as military service
retreat	to move back from an enemy attack to a safer location
stalemate	a situation in which further action is blocked and neither side in a conflict can win; a deadlock
strategy	the overall planning and conduct of large-scale military operations
tactics	actions or ways to achieve a goal or plans to win a battle

INDEX